COOL STUFF to PHOTOGRAPH

14 MEGA PIXELS

3x ZOOM f=6.6-19.8mm 1:3.2-5.9

Stephanie Turnbull

A+

Smart Apple Media

Published by Smart Apple Media, an imprint of Black Rabbit Books
P.O. Box 3263, Mankato, Minnesota 56002
www.blackrabbitbooks.com

U.S. publication copyright © 2015 Smart Apple Media.

Designed and illustrated by Guy Callaby
Edited by Mary-Jane Wilkins

With thanks to Mim Waller

Library of Congress Cataloging-in-Publication Data

Turnbull, Stephanie, author.
Cool stuff to photograph / Stephanie Turnbull.
    pages cm. -- (Cool stuff)
Includes bibliographical references and index.
Audience: Grade 4 to 6.
ISBN 978-1-62588-190-8
1. Photography--Juvenile literature. 2. Digital cameras--Juvenile
literature. I. Title.
TR149.T87 2015
770--dc23

                                 2013047370

Photo acknowledgements
t = top; c = center; b = bottom; r = right; l = left
page 1 taelove7/Shutterstock; 2 Jason Henry/Thinkstock; 4tr lanych/
Shutterstock; l and r Mim Waller, br strelov/Shutterstock; 5 Getty Images/
Thinkstock, tr Africa Studio, b Wendy Kaveney Photography/both
Shutterstock 6t Evgeny Karandaev, c YanLev, b bloomua/all Shutterstock; 7l
Robert Neumann/Shutterstock, r Kimberly Beck/Thinkstock; 8t Norman
Chan, c Edyta Pawlowska/all Shutterstock, symbols Nataliya Kostenyukova/
Thinkstock, b Tom Wang/Shutterstock 9t, c, b Mim Waller, br Krzysztof
Odziomek/Thinkstock; 10t STILLFX, tr, bl Mim Waller, br Lucky Irene/
Shutterstock; 11 tl, bl, bc, br Mim Waller, tr Renewer/Shutterstock; 12t
Aleksandar Mijatovic/Shutterstock, l, r, bl, br Mim Waller; 13tl jwblinn, tr
wong sze yuen/both Shutterstock, bl, br Mim Waller, 14c Ysbrand Cosijn, b
Omelianenko Anna; 15 t, c David Ionut, bl Tatyana Vyc, br stocker1970; 16t
Luba V Nel, l Jan Kratochvila, r johnbraid, br ID1974; 17t Peter Schwarz/all
Shutterstock, c Mim Waller, bl Jane Rix, br leungchopan; 18t Paul Vasarhelyi,
tl Dan Kosmayer/all Shutterstock, r amanaimagesRF, bl Igor Balasanov/both
Thinkstock, br Mim Waller, 19 bikeriderlondon/Shutterstock, tr Mim Waller,
b kavram; 20t MANDY GODBEHEAR, b bikeriderlondon; 21t Mat Hayward,
b tobkatrina; 22t Roman Gorielov/all Shutterstock, l Mim Waller, br
Belozorova Elena/Shutterstock, 23t Mim Waller, br Infoto; 24t Norikazu, tl
Alex Kosev, cl Matt Ragen, cr mountainpix, r Pongsak keerestanbut, plug
socket William J. Mahnken/all Shutterstock, bl, br Mim Waller; 25tl Orla,
tr Pinkcandy, c Suzanne Tucke, bl racorn, bc michaeljung; 26t Kamira/all
Shutterstock, bl, bl Mim Waller, r, br Guy Callaby; 27tr Marko Tomicic, tl
wherelifeishidden, r iofoto, bl, Pavel L Photo and Video, br Nolte Lourens,
scissors Coprid/all Shutterstock; 28 Mim Waller, 29 Mim Waller, br Mike
Red/Shutterstock; 30 Mim Waller; 31 Mim Waller; 32bl Anemone, bc
borzywoj, br bioraven/all Shutterstock
lightbulb in Cool Ideas boxes Designs Stock/Shutterstock
Cover 474344sean/Thinkstock

Printed in China by Imago Publishing
PO: DAD0058
PO Date: 032014

9 8 7 6 5 4 3 2 1

Contents

Snap Happy

It's fun to take photos, but it's even better when your photos are fantastic! You don't need years of training and an expensive camera–just a few skills and plenty of imagination.

Be Prepared

If you already have a camera, you probably use it on vacation and at parties, but photos can also capture great moments during ordinary days. Perhaps you spot amazing autumn leaves as you play in the park, or a joke that makes your friends laugh. Keep your camera handy, and you'll never miss a photo opportunity.

Everyday sights such as your friends walking to school or a tree standing against a clear sky can make striking photographs.

Cool Idea

Get into the habit of regularly uploading your photos on to a computer or flash drive so you don't accidentally delete great pictures.

Did You Know?

For many years, cameras produced images on plastic strips of film. The first digital cameras were invented in the late 1980s, but they cost thousands of dollars to buy.

Show Them Off

Take photos to be seen, not to stay in your camera! Send good shots to friends, or print and frame them as personalized gifts. Creating a **photomontage** or decorating your room with your best prints can also be fun.

Think First!

Before taking photos in public places, check to see whether photography is allowed. Some places prefer you to switch off the **flash**. Don't photograph people without asking first, and remember that your friends may not thank you for sharing unflattering photos online!

Which Camera?

Every digital camera works in the same way: you press the **shutter button**, which opens a hole to let light in, and then the light passes through a glass lens on to an electronic sensor. This forms the image and records it on a memory card.

Pixel Power

Images taken by digital cameras are made up of tiny dots called **pixels**. The bigger a camera sensor is, and the more pixels it has, the more detail it can show–which means better quality photos. Cameras with fewer pixels may produce images that look out of focus or blocky when printed.

Individual pixels show up as tiny squares of color. The more pixels in an image, the better quality it is.

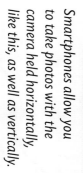

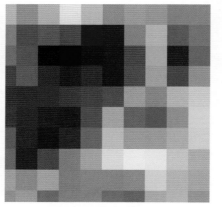

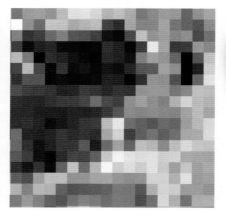

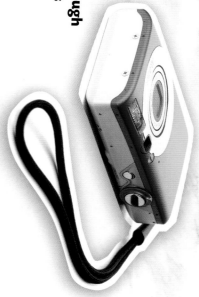

Camera Phones

The camera you're most likely to own is built into your cell phone or **smartphone**. Camera phones have very small sensors with about three, four, or five million pixels (megapixels), so images may look blurry, especially in dim light. But you can still take good photos!

Smartphones allow you to take photos with the camera held horizontally, like this, as well as vertically.

Compact Cameras

Compact cameras are small, fairly cheap digital cameras. They usually have sensors with between eight and fourteen megapixels, so they take better quality photos than cell phones. They're ideal for helping to improve your photography skills.

Compact cameras are easy to use and lightweight to carry. They come in different colors and styles.

Cool Idea

Don't forget that your cell phone or compact camera may also take short films with sound. Use this feature to capture fast-moving things which would be blurred in photos.

DSLR Cameras

Digital single-lens reflex (DSLR) cameras are the most expensive type of digital cameras. They have big sensors (ten to eighteen megapixels) and lenses that screw on and off for taking different types of photos, such as close-ups and night shots. DSLRs take high-quality, sharp photos...but you probably don't need one just yet.

Did You Know?

Compacts and cell phones don't really click when they take a photo–that's just a sound effect!

7

Getting Started

First of all, take time to learn how to use and look after your cell phone camera or compact camera. This will make it last longer and help you take better photographs.

Handle with Care

Cameras may look sturdy, but they contain intricate, fragile parts. Buy a case or cover to protect the screen from being broken or scratched. Don't let your camera get wet, and avoid dirt, dust, or sand that could damage the insides.

Holding your camera up in the air like this is bound to result in blurred or crooked shots!

Keep It Steady...

Practice holding your camera still to take photos. If you can, steady it with both hands, even if it's your cell phone. Brace your upper arms against your body, stand on both feet, and keep still for a second after taking the picture. There can be a slight delay before the camera takes the shot (called shutter lag), and you'll blur it if you move too soon.

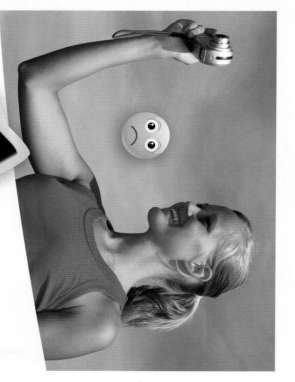

Camera cases can be hard plastic or soft, padded fabric, and they usually have a handy carrying strap.

Check Your Settings

Using your camera's special settings really improves your photos. One of the simplest and best is autofocus. First press the shutter button half way down. The camera will automatically focus and will beep when it's done. Press the button down fully to take the photo.

With autofocus

Without autofocus

Autofocus makes a huge difference! Without it, photos are slightly fuzzy because of the shutter lag, but with it they're much sharper.

Another useful tool is the close-up setting. This makes near objects stand out in sharper focus. Again, half press the shutter button to let the camera focus, and then press it right down.

With close-up setting

Without close-up setting

Cool Idea

Don't bother with the zoom button on cell phones, as it just enlarges the middle of the picture and reduces image quality. Instead, move closer!

Did You Know?

*You can buy all kinds of camera accessories, including **tripods** to keep cameras still, extra-powerful flashes, and even waterproof cases for underwater photography.*

The Right Light

Before you take a picture, check the light. Is the sun so fierce you can't see your subject, or is it dull and gloomy? Having the right lighting makes a huge difference in how good your photo will be.

Sun and Shade

Sunlight gives a warm glow that is more flattering than harsh indoor lights. But be careful—bright, direct sun can bleach out parts of your photo and cast dark shadows that blot out other areas altogether. Here are some top tips for taking cool photos on hot days.

1. Try to avoid midday sun. Experts take stunning photos in the early morning or late afternoon, when the light is softer. This makes colors richer and deeper.

2. Position people in a shady spot, such as under a tree. Shadows keep your picture from looking flat and washed out.

3. Make sure the sun is shining from the side. If people look into the sun, they squint, and if it's behind them, they'll be in silhouette.

These photos have a good balance of light and shade, giving the subjects a great glow. Don't be afraid to move around and try different shots.

Dark Days

The sensor in cell phone cameras and some compacts isn't powerful enough to take good photos in poor light, and the flash (if there is one) isn't always effective. Check your settings to see if there is a dim light or night shot mode. This keeps the shutter open longer as you take a photo. Movement will show as a blur, so keep extra-still, or rest the camera on a flat surface.

Reflected Light

Photographers often use **reflectors** to bounce light on to their subject and to soften the contrast between light and dark areas. Here's how to make one.

1. Find a large cork board. Crumple and then flatten sheets of tin foil, and wrap them around the back of the board. Pin the edges in place.

2. Position a light to one side of a friend and take their photo. Part of their face will be in shadow.

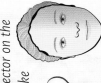

3. Prop the reflector on the other side and take the photo again. There should be less shadow.

Whiteboards, polystyrene panels, pale umbrellas, or white sheets also work well.

Without reflector

With reflector

Did You Know?

The earliest camera flashes used powder which the photographer lit to make it explode in a blaze of light.

Cool Idea

Why not take artsy photos of shadows?

Frame It

Before you take a photo, look at the image on your screen and imagine it in a frame. Does it really grab your attention, or is it cluttered and confusing? Choose carefully what you want to include in a photo and where you want it to appear.

Tall or Wide?

Does the image suit a **landscape** (horizontal) or **portrait** (vertical) shot? If in doubt, try both and decide afterwards which worked best. You might be surprised how different things can look when framed another way.

This portrait image (left) highlights details of the windmills and boat, while the landscape shot (below) gives a wider view of several windmills.

Did You Know?

Top-quality cameras can take photos in which the subject stands out in sharp focus, but the background is just a blur. For this they need a very wide aperture (hole).

Watch This Space

Decide what you want to focus on–your friend, a building, or something else–but don't forget the whole frame. Look at the area around your subject. If it's empty space, move in closer so your subject fills the frame better. If it's a very busy background, change your position to simplify things.

The shape and detail of this ornament (right) is lost against a busy background (top) but stands out much better in a clearer, lighter place (bottom).

Oops!

Checking the whole frame can help you avoid mistakes such as including an ugly wastebasket at the edge of a beautiful landscape or not noticing that a sign directly behind your friend seems to be growing out of his head!

Check your framing to avoid chopping off someone's head or including distracting background details.

Cool Idea

Find an old frame, remove the glass and photograph friends looking through it. Wow—instant framed portraits!

Think in Thirds

One technique used by photographers is called the rule of thirds. It's a great way of composing striking, professional-looking photos. Try it yourself, and see what you think.

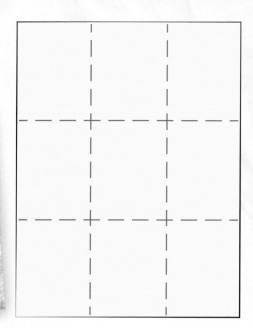

Did You Know?
The rule of thirds has been used by painters for centuries.

Split the Screen

First, imagine lines splitting your camera screen into thirds, both across and down.

Now move your camera so that the things you want to photograph are roughly along some of these lines. This makes your picture more interesting than it would be if objects were in the middle.

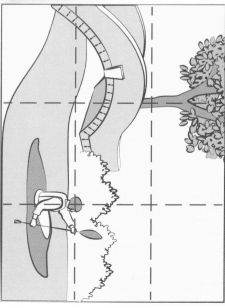

For example, this is a nice enough picture of your dog...

...but this one has a lot more energy and excitement, as it gives a better sense of the dog racing into the picture.

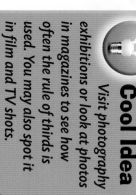

Cool Idea

Visit photography exhibitions or look at photos in magazines to see how often the rule of thirds is used. You may also spot it in film and TV shots.

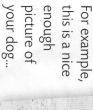

14

Make an Impact

The rule of thirds also helps to highlight important parts of a photo and makes them look more impressive. For example, a scenic photo with the **horizon** slicing the picture in half is OK...

... but moving the horizon to the upper third focuses attention on the beautiful sea.

Hot Spots

Think about the four points where the imaginary lines cross. These are sometimes called hot spots.

Try to place important objects (or parts of objects) on a hot spot. They will be far more noticeable here.

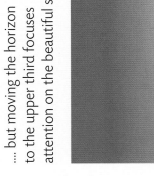

Cool Close-Ups

One common mistake is to stand so far back from your subject that everything looks very small and distant in the finished shot. Instead of trying to cram in a whole building or scene, get up close and pick out a detail–you can always take extra photos to capture the rest!

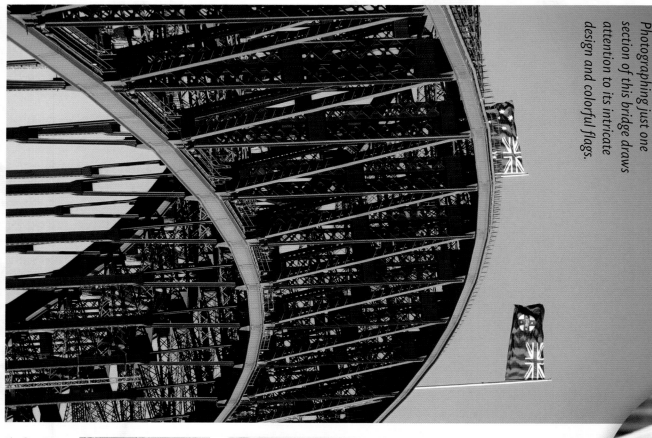

Photographing just one section of this bridge draws attention to its intricate design and colorful flags.

Perfect Position

Compact cameras are great for taking close-ups, as the lens focuses well when it is near to subjects. Use the close-up mode (see page 9), and position the subject carefully. You could use the rule of thirds (see pages 14–15) or center it and fill the frame completely.

Old buildings are covered in detailed shapes and patterns that make great photos.

Ordinary to Amazing

Once you start taking close-ups, you'll realize just how much there is to photograph! Things that seem very ordinary can look more interesting when you pick out one detail. Look around and see what you can spot.

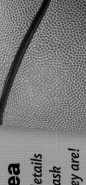

Fill the Frame

A photo filled with lots of identical objects can look great. Peer into a box of cookies, a jar of candy, or a plate of pasta, or hunt for leaves, pebbles, feathers, or grass. Get close and fill the frame with shapes and colors.

Cool Idea

Photograph details of everyday objects and ask friends to guess what they are!

Amazing Angles

If you want to surprise people with dramatic photos, don't just stand there–move! Change your position and the angle you shoot from to give your pictures more impact.

A Giant's View

Standing higher up–on a chair, or up steps–and looking down at your subject can give you an unusual viewpoint. It can show details or patterns you'd miss otherwise and create weird and wonderful size **distortions**.

Everyday things can be a lot more intriguing when viewed from above.

Be a Worm

Now try the opposite viewpoint. Crouch or lie on the ground and gaze up at your subject. Low angle shots often make people, buildings, or trees seem more impressive or important. They're also effective for photographing small subjects such as flowers.

Don't be afraid to lie on the ground–but keep the camera out of the mud!

18

Cool Idea

Try looking down at your feet and photographing them on interesting backgrounds.

Change it Up

Usually you want a straight horizon, but how about deliberately taking photos at funny angles? Try tilting the horizon and see how it can liven up an ordinary scene—or perhaps make people feel a little seasick!

Did You Know?

Fisheye lenses for DSLR cameras take very wide-angle photos, curving and distorting the lines to fit everything in.

People Pictures

One thing you'll definitely want to photograph is people. Follow these top tips to take photos of your friends that make everyone (including you) look their best.

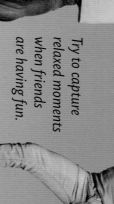

Try to capture relaxed moments when friends are having fun.

Great Groups

For group photos, look for good light (see page 10) and a clear, uncluttered background (see page 12). Move people close together, but don't pose them too rigidly, or they'll feel stiff and awkward. Chat and joke so everyone relaxes.

Don't have big gaps between people, like this—focus on them, not the whole room.

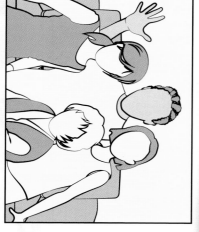

Making sure everyone's heads are close together creates a better shape and makes people sit or stand in a more casual way.

Props and Costumes

Remember that not everyone likes having their photo taken. Handing someone a prop gives them something to hold and focus on. You could provide some silly clothes, hats, sunglasses, and wigs to dress up in. While everyone's having fun, stand back and snap.

Some shots are bound to be blurred, or catch people blinking, so take lots!

Super Selfies

Taking self-portraits is a great way of practicing your photography skills. If you're using a compact camera, experiment with setting the timer. With a cell phone, try hard not to show your arm—it looks terrible!

Did You Know?

One of the first selfies was taken in 1914 by Anastasia, daughter of the last Russian emperor.
The 13-year-old used a mirror to take the photo and sent it to a friend.

Taking selfies is a chance to pull your silliest faces!

Cool Idea

Take more imaginative selfies by tilting the camera at an angle or photographing your reflection in a surface that distorts images, such as a car mirror or the back of a spoon.

Artsy Ideas

One cool way to use your camera is to focus on lines, curves, colors and textures. This **abstract** photography creates exciting images rather than showing what something really looks like.

This close-up of oil in water makes a wonderful abstract image.

Natural Art

Nature is full of amazing shapes and patterns all year around. Look for colors in fallen leaves, swirls in sand or snow, fantastic cloud formations, or patterns in pavement cracks. Don't try to include too much—your image will be more effective close up.

Study trees in your back yard or local park, and discover amazing textures in the bark.

Cool Idea

Take photos through rainy windows to create interesting blurry shapes and colors.

Guiding Lines

Another idea is to use the natural lines in a landscape (such as walls or roads) to guide your eye into the picture and towards something in the distance. This is a clever way of giving an image extra depth and a striking shape.

The photo above draws your eye to the cat and then beyond it, through the archway.

Mood and Feeling

When you take an artsy photo, think about the mood you want to convey. Is it a positive image bursting with life and color, or does it have a melancholy or mysterious atmosphere?

This photo could make you feel sad that the glove is lost or wonder who it belonged to.

23

Funny Faces

Great photos don't have to be serious. Get close to funny faces and snap photos that make you smile. Frame your best shots and display them—or send them to friends to give them a giggle.

Objects Alive!

Windows, doors, grates, and other features on buildings can look just like eyes and mouths. Go on a face-hunt and see if you can photograph objects with personality!

Frame your images carefully to avoid features that aren't part of the funny face.

Crazy Characters

If you can't find faces around you, try creating your own. All you need is a pair of googly plastic eyes. Stick the eyes on to everyday objects that look vaguely head-shaped, and take photos of your newly-created characters.

24

Cool Idea

Arrange fruit or vegetable pieces on a plain background to make a smiley face, and turn your photo into a cheerful greeting card.

Acting Up

Your friends and family probably have pretty funny faces themselves, so stand them in front of a blackboard and let them strike silly poses. Use chalk to draw funny speech bubbles or pictures around them and start snapping!

This is a good chance for your friends and family to try out their acting skills!

You could even tell a short story by changing the speech bubbles and positions for each frame. Print out the finished photos and display them in order.

Finishing Touches

There's more to photography than taking photos! Editing your shots on screen can give them a professional look. Try these tips and see the difference they make.

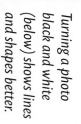

On-Screen Tweaks

Programs such as GIMP (available free online) and Adobe Photoshop are very useful for making small but effective changes, such as lightening parts of photos lost in dark shadow or getting rid of **red eye**, which happens when photos taken with a flash make people's eyes glow red.

Red eye (above) can spoil a photo, but it's easy to turn pupils black again using a computer.

Did You Know?

There are all kinds of **apps** to give photos fancy effects such as black borders, colored filters, or even outlines that make images look like cartoon drawings.

Turning a photo black and white (below) shows lines and shapes better.

26

Crops and Chops

Before printing photos, check your framing and use a **cropping** tool to reposition main features or slice off unwanted edges. Here are some general guidelines for cropping people–but don't worry if you sometimes break the rules. Go with what looks good to you!

3. It's usually OK to chop off the top of the head–but not the chin.

4. Watch for hands coming in from the side that don't seem attached to the body. The best thing to do is to cut them out altogether.

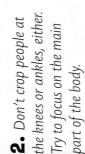

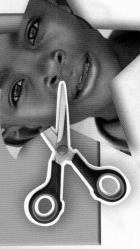

Cool Idea

Why not take a pair of scissors and crop photos by hand? Plan where to cut, and arrange your cut-outs to create a fun scrapbook, album, or wall display.

1. Try not to crop arms at the wrists or elbows, as it can look awkward.

2. Don't crop people at the knees or ankles, either. Try to focus on the main part of the body.

27

Camera-Free Photos

You don't always need a camera to take photographs. Here are two clever ways of creating cool images without switching on your camera!

Scanner Art

Scanners are great for close-up pictures. Anything touching the glass screen will produce a sharp, detailed image, while parts not in contact with the screen will blur. The effect can be fantastic!

1. Choose a fairly flat, clean object to scan, and position it on the screen. Be careful not to scratch or damage the screen.

2. Close the scanner lid to give your object a white background. For a colored background, lay a sheet of colored paper or card over the object first.

3. Scan the image. If it's too big for the cover to close fully, make sure you don't look at the bright light—it could hurt your eyes.

4. Save the image on the computer, and crop or alter it using photo editing software.

Cool Idea

Scan old, delicate photos to keep a copy of them.

Sun Prints

Light-sensitive paper is great fun. It changes color when exposed to sunlight, so any objects placed on top block the light and leave white shapes on the paper. Buy packs online or from specialty photography stores, and follow these easy steps.

1. Find objects with interesting shapes. Keys, coins, paper clips, buttons, and jewelry work well.

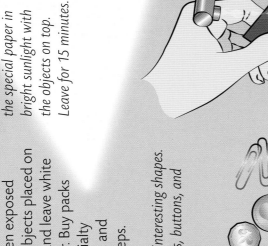

2. Place a sheet of the special paper in bright sunlight with the objects on top. Leave for 15 minutes.

3. Remove the objects and hold the paper under running water for a few minutes. It will turn dark blue except for the areas that were covered, which turn white.

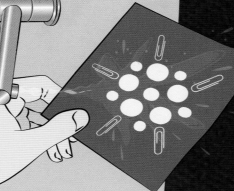

4. Let your print dry flat, and frame or display it.

Did You Know?

Images made on light-sensitive paper are called photograms. Artists use them to create stark, stylish images.

Glossary

abstract
Photography that doesn't try to show what ordinary objects, places, or people look like, but instead picks out striking colors, shapes and patterns.

app
Short for "application," a piece of software that can be downloaded to smartphones or computers. Some apps are free, while others must be bought.

cropping
Trimming a photograph so that only the most important or striking section remains.

distortion
A change in something that makes it look oddly different, such as being stretched or squashed.

flash
A device that creates a quick flash of artificial light to make a dull or dark scene brighter. Flashes are usually built into cameras, but some professional photographers use big, separate flashes to create lots of extra light.

horizon
The line where the land and sky seem to meet.

landscape
A shape of photograph wider than it is tall.

photomontage
A collage made from photos, or parts of photos, all stuck down together.

pixel
Short for "picture element," the smallest part of an image.

portrait
A shape of photograph taller than it is wide.

red eye
The effect of having glowing eyes in photographs. It happens when someone's pupils are wide in dim light, so the camera flash goes through them and reflects off the back of their eyes before the pupils have a chance to close up. Some cameras have a built-in red eye reduction, which is a flash before the photo is taken to make the pupils shrink.

reflector
A white, silver, or colored surface used by photographers. Many reflectors are lightweight, portable discs that fold away neatly.

shutter
The part of a camera that opens to let light through a hole and onto the sensor to take a photo.

smartphone
A cell phone that can also be used as a computer, with features including Internet access, games, music player, camera, and more.

tripod
A three-legged frame used to keep a camera in position. Some tripods have special bendy legs that can hold the camera at unusual angles for artsy shots.

Websites

Click it Up a Notch
www.clickitupanotch.com/2012/07/photography-for-kids
Check out this great, easy to read photography guide with helpful pictures.

National Geographic Kids—My Shot
http://kids-myshot.nationalgeographic.com
Look at lots of fantastic photos submitted by kids and get inspiration for your own.

10 Top Tips for Taking Better Photos With Your Cell Phone Camera
www.ephotozine.com/article/10-top-tips-for-taking-better-photos-with-camera-phones-18339
Find a list of handy hints and tips for taking photos with a cell phone camera.

Digital Photography for Kids
www.digitalphotography4kids.com/
Learn all about taking digital photos with this handy guide.

Index

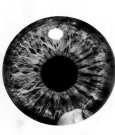